Most Powerful Healing Prayers by St. Padre Pio

Written By Saul Cross

Most Powerful Healing Prayers by St. Padre Pio

Copyright 2023. Motmot.org

All rights reserved. No part of this book may be reproduced or used in any manner without the prior written permission of the copyright owner, except for the use of brief quotations.

To request permission, contact the publisher by visiting the website: motmot.org.

Contents

A Note From the Author 6

The Life of Padre Pio 8

Intercessory Prayers 12
    The Most Powerful Healing Prayer by Padre Pio 16
    Prayer for Healing of Mind 18
    Prayer for Body Restoration 20
    Prayer for Spiritual Enlightenment 22
    Prayer against Sickness 24
    Prayer to Vanquish Fear 26
    Prayer of Surrender to God's Will 28
    Prayer for Strength during Illness 30
    Prayer for Clarity in Affliction 32
    Prayer to Stimulate Faith 34
    Prayer for the Healing of the Heart 36
    Prayer to Dispel Despair 38
    Prayer for Recovery from Disease 40
    Prayer for Healing after Loss 42
    Prayer for Courage in Suffering 44
    Prayer for Peace amidst Pain 46
    Prayer to Ease Gastric Ailments 48
    Prayer for Relief from Skin Maladies 50
    Prayer to Seek Serenity in Hospice 52
    Prayer against Insomnia 54
    Prayer for Harmony in Body and Soul 56

Prayer for Respite from Trauma ... 58
Prayer for Cleansing of Negativity ... 60
Prayer for Hope in Turmoil ... 62
Prayer for Renewal ... 64

Novena ... 68
   Introduction ... 69
   First Day ... 72
   Second Day ... 74
   Third Day ... 76
   Fourth Day ... 78
   Fifth Day ... 80
   Sixth Day ... 82
   Seventh Day ... 84
   Eighth Day ... 86
   Ninth Day ... 88

A Note From the Author

Dear Reader,

As a fellow Catholic, my heart felt an inexorable pull to delve into the spiritual stronghold of the humble friar, St. Padre Pio. Over the years, I've found myself comforted by his simple wisdom, invigorated by his uncompromising faith, and inspired by his steadfast dedication to God's divine grace. In times of sorrow, uncertainty, and sickness, I, like millions of others, have turned to St. Pio for guidance and intercession.

The prayers contained in this book, "Most Powerful Healing Prayers by St. Padre Pio," are an embodiment of St. Pio's lifetime of devotion, resilience, and love for our shared faith. Each prayer is a testament to his profound empathy for those suffering, his unwavering belief in God's healing power, and his unique ability to touch the souls of the faithful. They are gateways leading us closer to his spiritual essence, and above all, closer to God's infinite love.

These 25 prayers, and the powerful novena, are not merely words. They are heart whispers channeled from St. Pio himself, intermingled with the divine. They are an offering to God, an appeal for healing, and a balm to soothe the aches of the human soul. Each one aims to provide solace and strength, leading us towards inner healing and spiritual enlightenment.

As you walk this path of intimate prayer, let us remember that it is more than a mere recitation. It is a heartfelt conversation with God, a quiet listening for His voice within our hearts, and a humble step towards divine love and grace.

While it would indeed be a great boon to experience healing from our bodily ailments, the most profound healing, as St. Pio himself experienced and taught, is the inner healing of the soul.

This sacred healing develops through the authentic living of our faith, the humble acceptance of God's will, and the steadfast commitment to prayer.

I trust you will find, within these pages, a wellspring of faith that bears the potential to profoundly touch and renew your life. May these words nourish your soul, lift your spirit, and bring you closer to the most compassionate heart of God.

May St. Padre Pio watch over us and guide us on this remarkable journey of healing, faith, and spiritual discovery. It is my utmost hope that this precious saint's divine wisdom lights your path, and that the healing power of prayer brings peace into your life.

Yours faithfully,

Saul Cross

The Life of Padre Pio

In the humble land of Pietrelcina, Italy, 1887, came a child named Francesco Forgione who was bound to be an extraordinary figure in the realm of spirituality. He was destined to become none other than Padre Pio, a name that would become synonymous with healing, faith, and miracles in the Catholic Church.

From a tender age, the divine seed had been sown within Francesco. At five, he pledged his life to God, his heart burning with a divine fervor that set him apart from others. He was known for his frequent conversations with guardian angels and his deep-rooted love for prayer; these were the early signs of holiness blossoming within him.

His spiritual journey took an ascendant path when he joined the Capuchin monastery in Morcone. There, amidst other God-dedicated souls, Padre Pio's devotion eclipsed, lending an aura of reverence to his presence. In 1910, Francesco Forgione transformed into Padre Pio, imbued with the holy responsibility of priesthood. His Masses, steeped in profound contemplation, would often last for hours, drawing in scores of devoted followers.

A living embodiment of faith, Padre Pio surrendered completely to God's will, even accepting his inexplicable ailments as a divine directive. Then, in 1918, the heavens bestowed upon him an unprecedented grace – he manifested the stigmata, the very wounds of Jesus Christ. This miraculous phenomenon vaulted him further into the spiritual limelight. Pilgrims flocked to see him, seeking spiritual counsel and yearning for the miracles he was believed to perform.

Yet Padre Pio was not just a man of miracles; he was a beacon of piety and humility. He led a life of austere simplicity, abstaining from worldly distractions while persistently observing prayer, chastity, and poverty. His heart overflowed with compassion for the distressed, which led him to establish the hospital "The Home for the Relief of Suffering". He perceived the reflection of Christ within every soul, endeavoring tirelessly to dissipate their pain and suffering.

His final parting in 1968 saw him clutching a rosary and calling out to the Lord Jesus and Mother Mary. Despite his physical departure, his spiritual presence endured; he had declared that his true mission would commence after his death. Today, his influence looms larger than ever in the heart of the world.

Distinguished Popes recognized his divine sanctity; Pope Paul VI portrayed him as a man of prayer and suffering, and Pope John Paul II, who had sought Padre Pio's counsel in his younger days, canonized him in 2002. Presently, his resting place in San Giovanni Rotondo is venerated as a global pilgrimage site.

Padre Pio - Beyond his remarkable highlights as a seer, healer, and an embodiment of miraculous stigmata, he remains celebrated as a man of profound faith, resilience, and reverence. His life continues to be a grand testament to divine grace acting in unison with human will, reminding us all of the healing powers that abiding faith bestows.

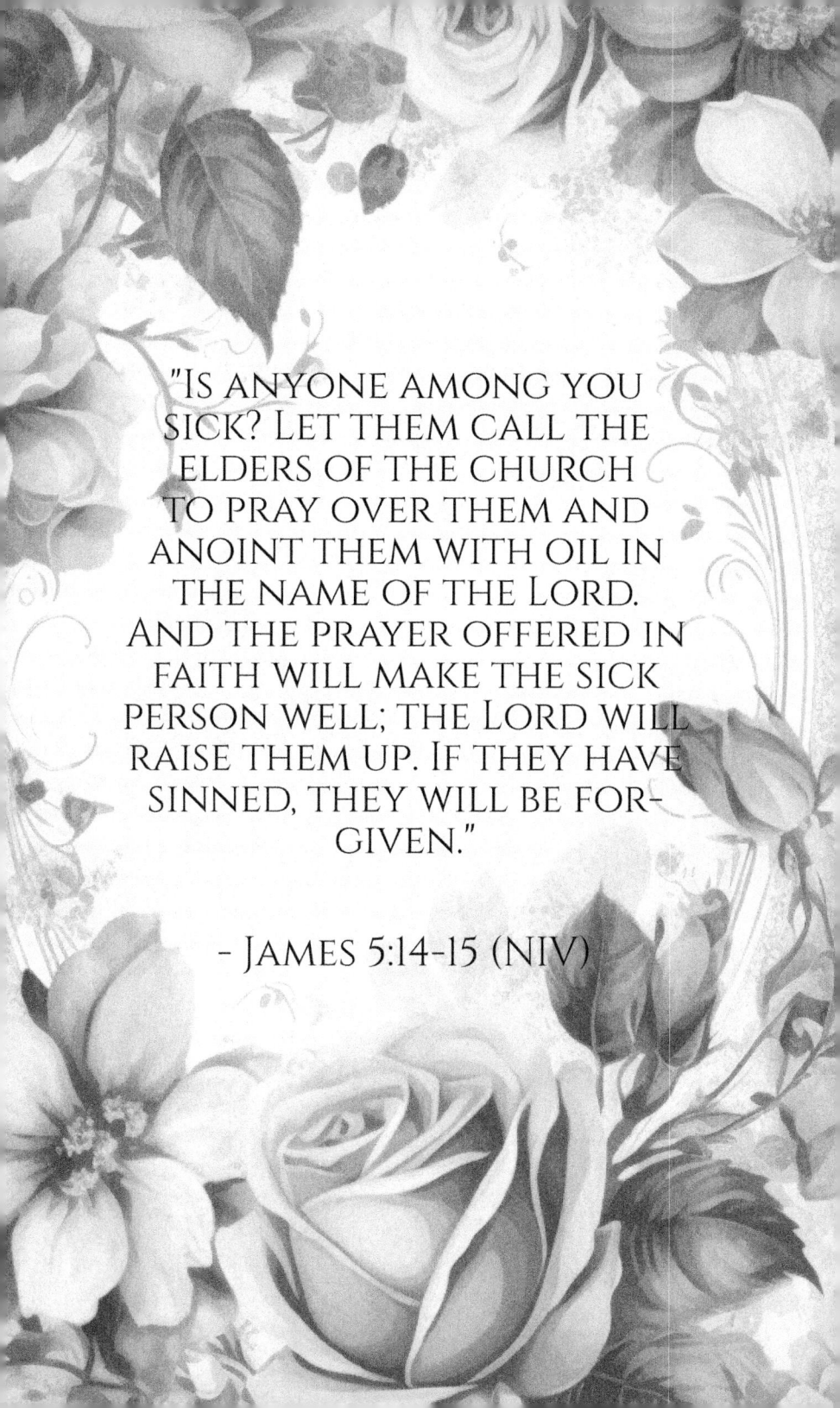

"Is anyone among you sick? Let them call the elders of the church to pray over them and anoint them with oil in the name of the Lord. And the prayer offered in faith will make the sick person well; the Lord will raise them up. If they have sinned, they will be forgiven."

- James 5:14-15 (NIV)

Intercessory Prayers

St. Padre Pio, referred to as the Mystic Monk, was a beacon of spiritual light for many. His life was a testament to the power of prayer and the healing grace that God bestows upon those who reach out to Him with faith and sincerity. This collection of prayers, seeking the intercession of St. Padre Pio, is meant to guide you on a journey of healing- physical, emotional, and spiritual. Each prayer has been composed with profound love and empathy, aiming to serve as a solace in times of turbulence and pain. The contents of the book span across a plethora of human experiences and woes, expertly woven into prayers that seek comfort and healing through divine intercession. Furthermore, they reveal the ever-prevailing truth that God is our biggest healer, and through Him, restoration is possible. This book is not just a collection of prayers, but a pathway leading you towards the divine grace and love of God, under the guidance and intercession of the beloved St. Padre Pio. So, open your heart, unfurl your spirit and allow the healing power of prayer to illuminate your path.

Thank you Lord for...

_____
_____
_____
_____
_____
_____
_____
_____

Padre Pio, intercede for me on...

_____
_____
_____
_____
_____
_____
_____
_____

Intercede for my loved ones...

_____
_____
_____
_____
_____
_____
_____
_____

My Personal Prayer

The Most Powerful Healing Prayer by Padre Pio

The prayer presented here was written by St. Padre Pio. It encapsulates his unwavering faith and trust in God's providence. The prayer begins with a profound gratitude for God's unfathomable love and the sacrifice of Jesus Christ, followed by a plea for healing in all dimensions – physical, emotional, and spiritual. The invocation of Jesus' precious blood signifies the redeeming power of Christ's sacrifice on the cross. As the prayer unfolds, Padre Pio interweaves his request for God's healing touch with a desire for an intimate union with Him. This prayer, like many of his writings, offers a mirror into the saint's soul – a testament to his profound spiritual journey and his role as a beacon of hope and healing.

Heavenly Father, I thank you for loving me. I thank you for sending your Son, Our Lord Jesus Christ, to the world to save and to set me free. I trust in your power and grace that sustain and restore me. Loving Father, touch me now with your healing hands, for I believe that your will is for me to be well in mind, body, soul and spirit.

Cover me with the most precious blood of your Son, our Lord, Jesus Christ from the top of my head to the soles of my feet. Cast anything that should not be in me. Root out any unhealthy and abnormal cells. Open any blocked arteries or veins and rebuild and replenish any damaged areas.

Remove all inflammation and cleanse any infection by the power of Jesus' precious blood. Let the fire of your healing love pass through my entire body to heal and make new any diseased areas so that my body will function the way you created it to function. Touch also my mind and my emotion, even the deepest recesses of my heart.

Saturate my entire being with your presence, love, joy and peace and draw me ever closer to you every moment of my life. And Father, fill me with your Holy Spirit and empower me to do your works so that my life will bring glory and honour to your holy name. I ask this in the name of the Lord Jesus Christ.

Amen.

Prayer for Healing of Mind

O Holy and Merciful St. Padre Pio, the divine healer of souls; bend thine ears of compassion towards us who besiege thy holy intercession.

Just as thou art beloved by our Heavenly Father; may thy love mirror upon us, especially those amongst us whose minds require thy healing touch.

As the darkness of confusion and despair shrouds our minds; we look to thee, who hath faced greater battles, and with thy faith emerged victorious.

Help us, oh kind and gentle saint; may thy experience guide our path towards healing and redemption.

We recognise our frailty, dearest Padre Pio; that within us lies the storm of thoughts, doubts, and fears.

Yet, we beseech thee, not in surrender, but with the hope born of divine love; intercede for us, oh blessed Padre, bring our pleas to the heart of the Divine Healer.

Amid the tempest of our minds, may we find shelter in thy holy intercession; just as the troubled found solace in your presence during your time on earth.

Let thy prayer, rich with thy wisdom and faith, brighten our gloomy minds; disperse the clouds of despair and let clarity shine upon us.

O humble servant of God, St. Padre Pio; thou who didst bear the divine stigmata, marking thy suffering and unity with our Lord;

may we also bear a mark, not of worldly pains, but a sign of heavenly comfort and divine consolation in our journey towards healing.

We yearn for restoration, St. Padre Pio; we are pilgrims seeking refuge, healing, and peace.

With thy holy intercession, may the most powerful healing touch of our Lord Jesus Christ restore our weary minds; fill our hearts with hope and our minds with his divine wisdom.

As the sunrise brings forth a new day; may each sunrise bring forth new hope in our hearts.

Comforted by thy prayers, may our faith be like the radiant dawn; dispelling the darkness, ushering the light of the healing mercy of our God.

To thee, St Padre Pio, we present our hopes; knowing thy understanding heart shall carry us in thy prayers.

Through thy holy intercession, may the healing love of Christ, like a soothing balm, calm our troubled minds; giving us strength, sustaining us in our journey towards wholeness.

In our desire for healing, we find strength in your intercession Padre Pio; let our prayer resonate with the echoes of your faith.

With the assurance of your intercession, we find hope; and in our hope, healing, for there in hope lies the true healing power of our Lord Jesus Christ.

In our plea, we implore not only for healing of mind but also a transformation of our hearts;

a healing that extends beyond the boundaries of the human mind and encompasses the entirety of our being.

And as we conclude our prayerful plea, we hold firm in our faith; knowing that through your holy intercession, Padre Pio, the most powerful healer, our Lord Jesus Christ, already bestows healing upon us. Amen.

Prayer for Body Restoration

Let me, St. Padre Pio, be the vessel of Your healing power.

Let my prayers be a conduit of Your restorative grace.

Let me trust in Your divine wisdom and compassion.

Let my faith be unyielding in the face of pain and adversity.

Let me not dwell on my sickness but on Your miraculous healings.

Let me not focus on my pains but on Your enduring love.

Let my heart keep a steadfast hope in Your power.

Let me surrender my worries and fears into Your comforting embrace.

Let my body be revitalized by Your touch.

Let my spirit find solace in Your healing grace.

Let every cell align with Your divine design.

Let me feel Your life-giving energy coursing through my veins.

Let me walk in wholeness, echoing Your perfect creation.

Let the shadow of sickness be vanquished by Your glorious light.

Let the chains of infirmity be shattered by Your might.

Let me rise from this infirmity, a testament to Your mercy and power.

Let my trial not weaken me but make me stronger in You.

Let my suffering not cloud my faith but illuminate Your presence.

Let my experience be a beacon, guiding others to trust in You.

Let me bear witness to Your healing, a testament of hope to those in pain.

Let my song be of thanks and praise for You, my Healer and Restorer.

Let me proclaim Your wonders to those yearning for Your touch.

Let my life, restored and renewed, be a praise to Your Name.

Let me serve You with all of my being, a channel of Your love to others.

Let my recovery be swift, my strength revitalized under Your care.

Let my spirit radiate Your peace, my body reflect Your perfection.

In the end let me, St. Padre Pio, be Your humble servant forever, healed, restored, and devoted to You, living testament of Your limitless love, power and mercy. In Your Holy Name, Amen.

Prayer for Spiritual Enlightenment

Dear St. Padre Pio, worthy servant of God,

In my struggles and sickness, I reach out to you for your intercession, for I am in need of the most powerful healing prayers known to mankind, ones you have made manifest during your time on earth.

When my body feels weak, frail and broken, intercede for me, dear Padre Pio, that I may find strength, healing, and wholeness in the divine grace of our Lord.

When my spirit is troubled, weighed down with worries, doubt, and fear, seek for me the light of spiritual enlightenment that pierces through every darkness.

When despair threatens to consume me, when it seems that hope has fled, pray for me, that I may be filled with unstoppable faith and an unwavering belief in God's infinite love and mercy.

During times of suffering, when pain becomes my constant companion, petition on my behalf that I can find comfort and solace in the crucified Christ, who purifies us through sufferings.

In moments of loneliness, when I feel abandoned and lost, help me perceive the comforting presence of our Lord, a presence that never leaves, never forsakes.

O St. Padre Pio, when the world around me seems devoid of compassion, nurture within me a heart that loves without measure, that heals through the power of divine mercy.

Through your intercession, I ask for a spirit that forgives readily, echoing the infinite forgiveness that our Lord extends towards mankind.

In times of difficulty, when I lack the courage to face the morrow, inspire within me resilience, a quiet courage that is born from a profound trust in God's plan for me.

St. Padre Pio, as you accompany me on my journey, remind me always of the blessed assurance residing within Christ's promises.

I ask this in faith, firm in the knowledge that healing flows from the wounds of Christ, the most powerful healer the world has ever known.

By your profound love for Jesus, intercede for me, St. Padre Pio, that I, too, may come to love Him more deeply and serve Him more faithfully.

Through your intercession, dear Padre Pio, may I realize that in losing myself to God's will, I find my true self, and by surrendering to His divine plan, I emerge victorious.

In surrendering, let me find freedom; in dying, let me find life; and in accepting my weaknesses, let me find true strength through Christ who strengthens me.

With a profoundly humble heart, I seek your intercession, St. Padre Pio. My faith rests not in my strength, but in the transformative power of God's healing grace, working through you.

Amen.

Prayer against Sickness

In the name of the Father, the Son, and the Holy Spirit; I seek thy holy intercession, St. Padre Pio.

Behold, I place before you my afflictions; may it be transferred to your sacred stigmata.

You, St. Padre Pio, who bore the wounds of Christ; I implore your divine plea.

You, who understand the pain of sickness; intercede for me in the court of Heaven.

I believe, with you, in the redemptive power of suffering; may my illness serve God's glory.

I believe, with you, in the healing touch of the Divine physician; pray that his hand may rest upon me.

You, to whom the Virgin Mary imparted the mystery of suffering; plead my cause to her immaculate heart.

Through the sorrowful passion of Jesus, and your shared affliction; I seek deliverance and comfort.

I trust, St. Padre Pio, in your prayerful intercession; for in Christ, peace is found amidst torment.

You, who know well the power of faith; strengthen mine in this time of trouble.

I believe, with you, in the Most Holy Sacrament; the source of healing and life.

You, who spent hours in adoration; intercede that I may draw strength from the Eucharist.

In communion with the suffering Christ and his sorrowful Mother; I surrender my infirmities.

Through your intercession, St. Padre Pio, may the Divine Physician's hands heal me; His mercy uplift me.

In the name of the Father, I ask; in the name of the Son, I hope; in the name of the Holy Spirit, I trust.

Amen.

Prayer to Vanquish Fear

O St. Padre Pio of Pietrelcina, you who bore the wounds of Christ in your flesh,

Let tears of healing rain down from heaven upon those in sickness and affliction.

Congregate us in fields of mercy, where petals of grace illuminate the shadows of our fears.

In the cauldron of despair, you stir hope, antidote to dread.

Teach our hearts to nest in the hollow of your hands.

May our sorrows yield fruits of compassion, as the tough husk of affliction breaks open to reveal the soft heart of understanding.

Be a lantern in our night, St. Padre Pio. As the doe longs for streams of water, our souls thirst for solace.

We beseech the revitalizing spring of your intercession, eroding mountains of fear into grains of trust.

May your healing touch, a console from on high, trace the contours of our afflictions, just as summer's breeze combs through autumn leaves.

Stir within our spirits an indomitable wind of fortitude.

May we, anchored in faith, find our solace not in the absence of storms, but in your unwavering presence throughout them.

O St. Padre Pio, your divine surgeon's hand crafted the tapestry of life.

Sew our wounds with threads of courage, and mend our ruptured spirits with the balm of divine remedy.

Guide us on the path of recovery, paved with stepping stones of hope and resilience, resting in the shadow of the Most

High.

Shepherd us through the abyss of fear, into pastures swathed in tranquility.

Illuminate our path with faith's lantern, dissolving the mist of apprehension.

Let our flesh be a canvas, where the artistry of divine healing forms masterpieces of restored health.

St. Padre Pio, cast your gaze upon our trembling hands and offer them rest in yours.

In your boundless compassion, dispel our fears and cradle us in the warmth of celestial comfort.

Speak serenity into the whirlwind of our distress, and quench our fear with the soothing balm of your holy reassurances.

Grant us eyes to witness the beauty in our trials and ears to hear the symphony of divine healing echoing throughout our lives.

With each rising sun, renew our spirits. And with each setting sun, may we find solace in the embrace of holy slumber.

May your healing prayers tenderly engrave the reassurances of faith in our hearts, St. Padre Pio.

Be our divine muse, and in your sanctuary of serenity, acquaint our voices with songs of celestial healing.

Be our beacon of hope amid our fears, and cradle us in your tranquil harbor, crowned by the light of the eternal.

St. Padre Pio, through your intercession, may we become vessels of divine grace, effervescing with resilience and serenity.

In your intercession, we seek refuge, for we know that fear shall no longer reign when heaven's love rains down upon us. Amen.

Prayer of Surrender to God's Will

O divine and merciful God, source of all healing and comfort; we seek Your mercy in our sufferings.

Saint Padre Pio, your life was a testament to the power of divine grace; intercede for us with your.Most Powerful Healing Prayers.

We are weary, dear saint; our bodies hurt; our spirits are low; we need the soothing balm of God's love; intercede for us.

In the face of sickness, we often feel helpless; yet we know, through God, all things are possible.

We ask for healing, dear saint; not just of body, but of mind and spirit; lead us on the path towards wholeness.

Oh saintly Padre Pio, we trust in your prayers; we believe in the power of our God; pray for us, that we may find comfort.

We surrender our desires, our hopes, our anxieties; thus, we trust in His divine plan.

God's way isn't always clear to us; yet we know He is our loving Father; remind us of His mercy, dear saint, in our darkest moments.

When pain overshadows joy; when doubt creeps into our hearts; may your intercession strengthen our faith.

The disease seems insurmountable, yet we persevere; fortified by your prayers, dear Padre Pio.

Life's tribulations may test us; yet, in God, we find our refuge; pray for us, dear saint, to remain strong in our faith.

We feel the weight of our sins; they burden us; in God's infinite mercy, we ask for forgiveness and healing.

In bodily suffering, we find a share in Christ's passion; Padre

Pio, help us to see; to unite our sufferings with His.

Through your intercession, dear saint, may we experience the healing power of God's love; easing our ailments, soothing our worries.

In God, we place our trust; may His will be done; this reality, may we humbly accept.

May His divine mercy flow unto us; healing our bodies, comforting our souls, strengthening our spirits.

Through your intercession, Padre Pio; may we commit to a life in Christ; filled with love, faith, and surrender.

As you bore the stigmata, dear saint, teach us to bear our crosses with love; finding grace in suffering; hope in despair.

Dear Padre Pio, pray for us; intercede on our behalf; may His divine light guide our path.

In His divine will we find peace; help us surrender; align our hearts to His divine rhythm.

O Lord, You promise comfort to the afflicted; the healing balm for the weary; may we rest in Your divine embrace.

Strengthen us, oh Padre Pio, in our resolve; to persevere, to trust, to surrender.

Pray for us, dear saint, that we may surrender our will, our fears, our cries; to the divine healer, Redeemer of our souls.

In Him, we place our hope; Him, our healer, our comforter; O divine and loving God, Your will be done. Amen.

Prayer for Strength during Illness

Father in Heaven, shower Thy strength upon us; in the midst of illness, we seek Your healing light. Through the intercession of St. Padre Pio, we ask for his prayers to guide us in our time of need.

In the face of disease and weakness, remind us, O Lord, of our strength; the strength that resides beneath our human frailties. Even in our vulnerability, we are braced by the courage you instill within us; may it rise like a dawn within our hearts, illuminating the path to recovery.

Lord Jesus, in Your mercy, we find refuge; behold, we present our afflictions as an offering to You. Let it be not our burdens, but instead, stepping stones; stepping stones towards a deeper understanding of Your love and mercy. Each discomfort endured, a testament to our faith in You.

St. Padre Pio, intercede for us in our prayers; carry our pleas to the Throne of Grace. With you as our heavenly intercessor, we stand resolute; our suffering pales against the promise of Your Holy Healing.

O Savior, Your healing touch brings life to the barren and strength to the weak; guide us from our pain, lead us to Your peace. In fatigue and weariness, we find our strength in You; Your ceaseless love is our sanctuary, our resting place.

In moments of doubt, whisper to our hearts, O God, of Your unwavering presence. Remind us of the Miracles of Your Healing Hand; the whispered prayers that have moved mountains, the petitions that have broken chains. Through the intercession of St. Padre Pio, may we experience the miracles of your healing power.

Dear Father, bind up our wounds, soothe our pain; for in our suffering, we cling closer to You. Every tear shed, every cry uttered, strengthen our faith; for in our helplessness, You are our undeniable strength.

St. Padre Pio, our friend in Heaven, look upon us with pity; carry our weak prayers, elevate them with your own. In this communion of spirits, O Lord, we seek healing; not solely for our bodies, but, crucially, for our hearts and minds.

Finally, we affirm our unwavering faith in Your healing power, O Divine Physician. Strengthened by Your love, bolstered by the strength that flows from the prayers of St. Padre Pio; we are confident in our journey towards healing.

Lord, we surrender our burdens to You; grant us strength in our weakness and healing in our illness. With You, O Lord, all things are possible; and through the prayers of St. Padre Pio, may we bask in the glory of Your healing touch. Amen.

Prayer for Clarity in Affliction

O Most Holy St. Padre Pio, channel of divine mercy, bearer of the stigmata, faithful servant of the Lord,

In this time of affliction, we approach your mantle of grace, seeking your powerful intercession.

With hearts heavy with doubt, we plead for wisdom, illumination, understanding in our suffering.

Your own trials mirrored the Passion of Christ, yours a story of surrender, obedience, a testament to resilience.

Intercede, St. Padre Pio, for clarity in our affliction.

Project light onto our path, disperse the mists of bewilderment enveloping our minds,

We long for healing, an end to suffering, a reprieve from our burden.

St. Padre Pio, beacon of healing, you who have felt the wounds of Christ,

Kindle our faith, disseminate calm in the stormy sea of our afflictions.

May we recognize God's grace amidst our trials, may we glimpse His mercy in our despair.

Intercede, St. Padre Pio, that we may understand the divine mystery in our afflictions.

Speak to us, whisper solace and courage, fortify us with patience, pave our way with hope.

May we never falter, never surrender to despair, always cleave to the promise of God's triumphant love.

St. Padre Pio, splendid healer, through your divine intercession we seek relief.

May the balm of God's grace soothe our wounds, restore wellness, strength and joy.

May our hearts echo with the rhythms of divine vitality, our bodies inhabited by celestial serenity.

Intercede for us, St. Padre Pio, that with the touch of God's hand, our afflictions may dissipate.

May we sail courageously across the sea of suffering, anchored by faith, propelled by divine mercy.

Anoint us with hope, invade our despair with divine light, transform our trials into triumphs of grace.

In this season of healing, St. Padre Pio, lend us your spiritual strength,

Implore God's mercy on us, His divine healing over every affliction, over every pain and sorrow.

Upon the cross of our afflictions, may we find redemption, may our suffering illuminate a path to sanctification.

Amen.

Prayer to Stimulate Faith

Beloved St. Padre Pio, intercede for us in our hour of need.

In this life, when I stumble, may I arise stronger in faith through the power of your healing prayers.

In times of sickness, may I be healed; in times of despair, may I find hope through your divine intercession.

When overshadowed by fear, may courage take its place and ignite my faith.

When I am weak, may your prayers strengthen me and keep me steadfast.

Dear St. Padre Pio, when my faith wavers,

I pray that through your healing intercession it may stand firm.

When doubts cloud my mind, may I be given the grace to believe beyond what I can see.

Where there is unbelief, let there be strong faith.

St. Padre Pio, through your intercession, be my guide in this journey of faith.

In the dim light of trials, may your powerful healing prayers inspire me to bolster my faith.

When my path is unclear, guide me toward the light of unwavering faith.

Dear intercessor, St. Padre Pio, on days when faith seems distant,

I pray your healing prayers may draw me closer to unwavering belief.

When my heart is filled with uncertainty, may my trust in the Almighty's plan be rekindled.

Through your powerful intercession St. Padre Pio,

When my soul is weary, may it be rejuvenated with the invigoration of deep-rooted faith.

When my spirit is broken, may your prayers mend it with the serenity of steadfast belief.

Blessed intercessor, in moments when I feel unloved,

I pray your healing presence may remind me of the undying love of our Creator.

That through your intercession, I may feel His adoration, even in the solitude of my despair.

St. Padre Pio, when I am tempted to surrender to my fears,

Inspire me to rise above, having faith that every challenge only brings me closer to my Divine Creator.

When faith is hard to find, through your intercession, may it never cease to shine in my heart.

In the midst of my faults, let your prayers remind me of the beauty of redemption.

When the world seems unfair, may your intercession reassure me that the Lord's justice is always supreme.

In moments of sorrow, let your powerful healing prayers comfort me,

And in moments of joy, may they amplify the gratitude in my heart. St. Padre Pio, through your intercession, in times of darkness,

May your healing prayers ignite the glow of faith in me, guiding me back to the unending love of our Creator.

When I feel abandoned, may your prayers remind me of His eternal presence.

I ask this through your intercession, St. Padre Pio. Amen.

Prayer for the Healing of the Heart

Dear loved and loving St. Padre Pio, intercede for us; seek divine grace for our hearts, troubled like the sea in storm.

Hear our plea, O beloved St. Padre Pio, as we stand at the threshold of healing and renewal; beseech the Lord for us, for our hearts yearn for comfort. Guide us through the arduous journey of healing; let every beat of our hearts echo the rhythm of God's love, the rhythm that pardons, the rhythm that heals.

In our moments of desolation, remind us, St. Padre Pio, of the sacred beauty of life; of the persistent hope that thrives hidden within, even in the thickest darkness. In our moments of frailty, encourage us that within our stumbles are lessons engraved; let fall the scales from our hearts, so we may see with eyes of faith, with hearts purified by contrition.

Transmit into our hearts, St. Padre Pio, a sense of God's divine mercy; a mercy that heals, a mercy that transforms. Let us experience the touch of Christ in our hearts, let us feel warmth in His kindness, strength in His forgiveness. O St. Padre Pio, intercede for us, bridge our fallible human hearts with the divine heart of Christ, the heart most unconditional, the heart most compassionate.

Pray for us, St. Padre Pio, as we journey through valleys of shadows; advocate for us as we traverse through healing both seen and unseen. Appeal for us, as we confront our fears; plead for us, as we surrender our guilt. There is healing in admitting our brokenness; there is liberation in recognizing our weakness.

Implore for us, dear St. Padre Pio, that we embrace God's will without reservation; that we surrender ourselves, not to the chains of past afflictions, but to the promise of future glory. We long for healing, Lord; we desire peace. We thirst for you, O Christ; we hunger for your holy word. Guide us, St. Padre Pio; accompany us on this journey.

We are vessels, Lord, molded by the divine potter; we are the clay, you are the artist. Refine us in Your crucible of love; shape us with Your divine and loving hands. O St. Padre Pio, beseech this prayer for us; for from our hearts springs forth life, from our hearts flows faith, from our hearts emanates love.

May we journey this path of healing, with hope like the dawn, faith as firm as mountains, and love as deep as the sea. With hearts alleviated, spirits rejuvenated, let us echo: All is grace.

St. Padre Pio, intercede for us; for your heart understands our heart. And may our hearts be aligned with God's heart, now and forevermore. Amen.

Prayer to Dispel Despair

St. Padre Pio, servant of God and shepherd of souls, today I call upon you for your heavenly intercession.

In this realm of pain and despair, I feel lost and weary, stumbling in the dark. But with your guidance, may I find strength to walk in the light.

In moments when sickness seizes the body and wound the spirit, when affliction blurs my vision, may your intercession guide me towards healing and clarity.

Through turmoil and fear, I fear the breaking of my spirit. Yet, through your powerful prayers, may the Divine Love mend my heart, banishing fear with courage, replacing turmoil with peace.

Amid periods when loneliness whispers, seeking to make a home in my soul, & frailty threatens to consume me, St. Padre Pio, intercede on my behalf that I may experience companionship in solitude and mighty fortitude in weakness.

When faith falters, when doubt looms like a forbidding shadow, may your devout supplications renew my faith, shining light into my soul's darkness releasing me from the chains of skepticism.

As despair attempts to snuff out hope, and bitterness seeks to poison my heart, may your intercession inspire hope, transforming bitterness into forgiveness, despair into trust.

St. Padre Pio, through mistakes where sin stains my soul turning my path astray. May your intercession direct me toward remorse, guiding me back to God's grace.

In times when suffering becomes all too familiar, a silent partner I did not ask for. In your intercession, may I find solace, transforming suffering into a bridge leading to divine mercy.

Through the seasons of trials when it feels like life is a series of tribulations, may your prayers turn these trials into triumphs, these tribulations into blessings.

St. Padre Pio, in your wisdom, you taught us that, as we give, so shall we receive. As we forgive, we obtain pardon. As we are born, so shall we die. And with death, begins life.

In these testing times, pray for us, beloved saint, so that through your intercession, we may turn despair into hope, pain into healing, and death into a new life.

In the name of the Father, the Son, and the Holy Spirit. Amen.

Prayer for Recovery from Disease

Padre Pio, you who bore the wounds of Christ, we call upon your intercession. Let your voice echo in the divine chambers, we beseech weeblings on unknown tides, journeying through the vale of distress.

In favor of the storm-borne, we plead. Stand as beacon among the stars, guide the souls set adrift in the ravenous sea of malady. Be our lantern amidst the encircling gloom, the tempest roars and faith shivers, under your gaze, may fear wither.

In the vast expanse of sorrow, we entreat. Draw strength from celestial territories, let fortitude rain upon those besieged by disease. In every drop of torment they endure, let relief be distilled, under your patronage, may pain be stilled.

In the heart of tumult, we beseech. Breathe courage into the afflicted, those descending into the abyss of despair. Gird their spirits, anchor their hearts, under your mantle, may hope start.

In the cochleae of divine providence, we implore. Whisper our petitions, let cries for healing reverberate. Sear our pleas into the celestial scroll, under your advocacy, may restoration unroll.

You who bore the wounds of the Redeemer, we invoke. Spread your blessed intercession, blanket the afflicted with divine protection. When fears rise like surges, when doubts dive like anchors, under your intercession, may peace be the conqueror.

In the haven of divine favor, we plead. As the evening star kisses the twilight sea, let the glow of recovery dawn upon those in misery. Under your name, may health reclaim.

In the ends of our tether, we pray. Let love be their compass, grace their sail, faith their anchor in this gruelling trial. As waves crash, storms whirl, under your intercession, let hearts be still.

Padre Pio, you who mirrored the agonies of the Crucified, we beg. In the face of the life's tempest, be our lighthouse. Cast your vigilant eye upon us, under your watch, may healing be victorious.

In the altar of divine compassion, we implore. Ignite in us the flame of hope, let it burn bright to dispel the shadows of sickness. Under your watch, may solace spark.

Each plea, each tear, each sigh of despair, may it be cradled in your intercessory prayer. Like tender lighthouse beams piercing the night, under your intercession, may healing ignite.

To love, to hope, to courage, to strength, we dedicate our plea. May the dawn of healing rise, under your intercession, may divine mercy suffice. Padre Pio, wave-tossed we may be, but in faith, we stand firm, under your intercession, we affirm.

Prayer for Healing after Loss

O most merciful Lord, Your love wraps the universe in its grand tapestry; all tangled threads and beautiful patterns are in your gentle hands.

You've given this world St. Padre Pio, a beacon of such divine love, that even in his frail human form, he radiated your powerful healing energy. Now, sublime Father, I call upon his kind intercession and beg for your mercy.

The loss has created a void; deep darkness surrounds me, as the bright light of my loved one has been extinguished. My heart cries daily; sings a mournful song, a lament for the departed. But even in this sorrow, O Lord, I remember St. Padre Pio, who reminds us that you are infinite love, even when we see only emptiness and pain.

O gentle Savior, guide me through this darkness, as you guided our dear St. Padre Pio. Allow his words of hope to fill my desolate heart; let his powerful prayers for healing bring me comfort.

My body trembles in agony; my spirit is weak. My Lord, I trust in your grace. Just as St. Padre Pio entrusted himself to your divine will, so do I surrender my pain to your healing touch.

By the remarkable life of St. Padre Pio, allow me to be drawn closer to you, O God. Let his humble intercession guide me; his faith, an example of pure love for you, be my beacon. And through this loss, let my suffering be transformed by your divine healing, just as darkness yields to the dawn's first light.

My soul languishes in loss; yet I turn to you, ever the Comforter of the afflicted. Soothe my broken heart; dry my tears just as you consoled your humble servant, St. Padre Pio during his earthly toils. Allow me to find solace in your divine mercy, for in your caring embrace, O Lord, we find our true home.

And as St. Padre Pio intercedes on my behalf, I ask him to whisper my pleas to you, O Lord, for you hear all prayers uttered within the silence of our souls. May his prayers, so pure and powerful, find favor in your divine court and bring healing upon my weary soul.

O sublime Creator, my strength is found in you alone. Through the blessings of St. Padre Pio's intercession, grant me the courage to abide in this loss; to live in the shadow of this pain and yet see your ever-present light.

And like St. Padre Pio, who loved you in sorrow and joy, I will continue to faithfully serve you, O Lord; through each tear and each smile, knowing well that you, in your infinite wisdom and compassion, do weave a beautiful tapestry of life, even with the threads of loss.

With the heart of St. Padre Pio and the love of you, O Lord, I journey onwards, held by your grace and guided by your divine light. Amen.

Prayer for Courage in Suffering

Father of Compassion, through the intercessions of St. Padre Pio, we beseech Your healing touch onto our lives and those whose sufferings bear hard on their hearts. St. Padre Pio, a friend to the infirm and the diseased, we implore your intercession.

May we never forget the power of Your mercy, even when we are weak. Let us feel in our hearts the burden of our brothers and sisters, and in doing so, become more like Christ. Enlighten our minds, that we may perceive the path to healing and wholeness.

Let the weary find strength in their fragility, and the wounded your balm of healing love. May the promise of Your everlasting Love bring consolation to our hearts. Let sickness not dampen our spirits, but uplift them in a testament of faith in to Your Divine Providence.

Let us not be overcome by fatigue, but find restoration in You. Let sustenance be the gift that restores flesh and fortifies spirits. Let the faithful trust in the medicines administered and the hands that serve to heal in Your Name.

Let no ailment cause despair, but a renewed hope in Your saving grace. When we are anxious, may the peace that surpasses all understanding be the rock on which we stand. When pain persists, may we remember the wounds of our Savior.

Let courage be the banner of every soul in suffering. Let us drink from the cup of suffering with faith, knowing in suffering we share a fraction of what was borne by Christ Himself. Let the ill remember they are not abandoned, their pain and anguish seen, their tears counted.

Through St. Padre Pio's intercession, let the steps towards

miraculous recovery begin to rhythm with the beat of faithfulness. Let the weak be given strength, let the sick be given health. Let all who suffer feel your comforting presence.

Father, St. Padre Pio bore in his own body the wounds of Christ. In union with him, may we bear in our hearts a deep trust in Your healing power. It is in our humanity, our fragility, that you are made manifest. Show in our suffering your unfathomable Love.

St. Padre Pio, who shared in Christ's suffering, intercede for us. Obtain for us the grace we need to endure our own trials. Help us to see the value within our suffering, and to offer it for the salvation of others.

May the love of The Divine Physician reign in our hearts, casting out all fear. May the sick experience Your healing touch and feel the warmth of Your love. St. Padre Pio, pray for us that we, too, may bear our cross with courage. Allow our sufferings to draw us closer to the heart of Christ.

Father, hear our prayer for healing and transformation. Through the intercession of St. Padre Pio, let healing and hope emerge from hardship, and strength from suffering. May Your miraculous healing hand touch all those in need and may we be ever thankful all our days. Amen.

Prayer for Peace amidst Pain

Ocean of Mercy, as waves of pain crash in, let the healing prayers of St. Padre Pio be our beacon in the night. Let his intercessions weave a mantle of calm amidst the storm we endure, a stillness at the heart of turbulence.

Unseen Harbor, where our mortal vessels find no berth, hear our pleas spoken through St. Padre Pio. Let his whispered ordinances be the echo in our heart's grotto, a call to anchorage, a promise of the healing to come.

Silent Thunder, that rumbles beneath our hurts and fears, may St. Padre Pio's invocations strengthen us. Let these powerful healing prayers quiet the thunder, turn the storm into a sigh, a sacred susurration of healing winds.

Keeper of the Lighthouse, we, too often lost and wandering, seek the glow of St. Padre Pio's intercessory care. Let this radiant guidance from his prayers bathe our sorrows in heavenly light, make each painful tear a prism of Your divine love.

Navigator of Souls, steer us through these frothing waves of distress with the map of St. Padre Pio's orisons. Let his prayers bespeak our longing for Your healing, crafting compass roses from our aches, leading us towards Your sanctuary of peace.

Star above Mariner's Madness, we navigate a sea of endless night, let St. Padre Pio's prayers be our Polaris. Let his supplications trace the constellations of our healing journey, guiding our silent ship towards dawn, towards hope's first light.

Merciful Commander, hear our prayer through the intercession of St, Padre Pio. Speak to us in symptoms and dreams, reign victorious in our bodily battleship, carry us forth on an undercurrent of faith, to waters serene and shores bright.

O, Healer of the Tempest-tossed, align our heartbeat with the rhythm of St. Padre Pio's powerful healing prayers. Transform our human frailty into divine resilience, fortitude from faith, skins of iron cloaked in a gentleness divine.

Recall us, O Divine Mariner, to the dock of love even as the storm of pain rages. Help us find courage through St. Padre Pio's intercessory prayers, healing in heart's quiet harbor, and peace amidst life's pain. May those prayers gird us as we dance with the waves, hand in hand with grace, stepping on the music of celestial peace.

Master Navigator, chart us a path in these turbulent waters, and through St. Padre Pio's prayers, let us find the courage to sail. May we move forward, armed with hope, buoyed by love, guided by faith, to arrive at the tranquil shores of Your sweet relief.

Heavenly Healer, in whose hands rest the cure to all pain, prove yourself once more through the intercession of St. Padre Pio. Pull us back from the crashing waves of pain towards a shore bathed in celestial light. Adorn us with crowns of tranquility, and clothe us in robes of peace, for we are Your children, lost at sea, and earnestly seeking Your gentle embrace.

Prayer to Ease Gastric Ailments

Let me find rest in You, Most Divine Healer, as I battle this pain within me.

Make my body a temple of your healing love, and rid me of this gastric ailment.

Set Your gentle touch upon my distressed organ, sealing the cracks of damage within me.

Let me lean on Your strength, St. Padre Pio, in my moments of weakness.

As I walk through these days of discomfort, bear my troubles with me.

Lift me high on your wings of compassion, carrying me beyond my sorrow.

Let me feel Your soothing balm, God of Restoration.

Ease my pain, still my worries, and quieten my restless body.

Only Your divine love can calm the storm brewing in my belly.

Let me breathe in Your hope, Servant of God, St. Padre Pio.

Replace my suffering with serenity, my agony with tranquility.

May Your healing light shine bright within me, dispelling all darkness of disease.

Let me hear Your words of comfort, Greatest Comforter,

Whisper in my ear the melody of healing and the hymn of health.

Speak strength into my weary soul and resilience into my frail flesh.

Let me taste the sweetness of recovery, St. Padre Pio, through your intercession.

May my meals nourish and heal, not aggravate and inflame my condition.

Let the fruits of your miracles rejuvenate me and repair my wearied body.

Let me see Your work in me, Divine Physician, through the hands of those who treat me.

In every pill and every procedure, let me discern Your loving intent.

Guide them to diagnose correctly and treat me with precision.

Let me believe, dear St. Padre Pio, in the power of prayer and divine healing.

Fortify my faith that I may accept my circumstances as they are, not as I wish them to be.

Even in my lowest moments, let me sense Your comforting presence beside me.

Let me give thanks for healing that will come, in Your divine timing and perfect plan.

Give me the patience to endure, secure in the belief that my healing is on the horizon.

For in every affliction, there lies a blessing, hidden yet destined to emerge.

Through the intercession of St. Padre Pio, let my plea reach You, O Heavenly Father.

Amidst the clamor and strife, let my humble prayer rise to You.

Seeking Your divine mercy, favor, and healing, I knock at Your door.

With faith unwavering and hope abiding, I plead for my healing – in body, mind, and spirit.

Prayer for Relief from Skin Maladies

In your loving mercy, St. Padre Pio, I come before you. My skin aches, it burns; its affliction weighs me down, heavy as a stone. Hear my humble plea.

In your compassion, intertwine my suffering with yours, St. Padre Pio. As your own flesh bore wounds, so my skin bears its own affliction. I bow my tiresome body, anguished and weary, and lay it at your feet. Share with me your strength.

Turn your gentle gaze upon me, Padre Pio. Feel my distress, feel my pain. Let it move your heart, powerful in its devotion. Let your sacred wound, once a mark of suffering, become my beacon of hope.

Unite my affliction with your Passion, St. Padre Pio. Propel my plea higher, carry it to the heavens where divine healing dwells. Implore from the Almighty that fountain of mercy to anoint my skin, to soothe my discomfort. Pray for me.

As the dawn breaks through the night, break through my suffering, St. Padre Pio. Interrupt my distress with your gentle intercession. Summon from divine halls the soothing balm of divine healing upon my weary skin.

Lift my heart, unburden my spirit, spirit so weary from constant battle. Let the salve of divine mercy touch my skin, transforming my pain into relief, my suffering into redemption. Appeal to heaven on my behalf.

Oh, St. Padre Pio, carry my prayer to the throne of grace, let it resonate with the divine melody. Let it awaken the mercy of the Highest, the ultimate healer. Let His healing light touch my skin, renewing each cell, restoring every fiber.

As the rains replenish the parched earth, let divine mercy replenish my afflicted skin. Let it cleanse, let it restore, let it heal. Form my plea into a healing balm, St. Padre Pio, and anoint my skin.

By your intercession, St. Padre Pio, I yearn for relief. Implore the divine healing hand to descend upon me, to touch my skin, to drive away this malady. Amid my affliction, bear my plea upwards.

With hope, I await divine healing, certain in my heart that relief will dawn. Through your intercession, St. Padre Pio, my plea ascends, reaching out for divine mercy. In His compassion, may healing abound.

I thank you, Padre Pio, for your tender care. For transforming my plea into an anthem of hope. For being a bridge linking my suffering to divine mercy. Until relief arrives, stand by me.

Amen.

Prayer to Seek Serenity in Hospice

In the still halls of hospice, St. Padre Pio we seek your intercession.

In quiet corners where pain resides, we ask for the comfort of the Most Powerful Healing Prayers.

Through open windows where light slants in, in shadows where darkness creeps, we ask for the warmth of God's healing touch.

On soft pillows where rest is sought, on hard floors where restless feet tread, we plead for the serenity only God can provide.

In whispered conversations that carry weight, in silent ones meant only for God's ears, we seek your intercession, St. Padre Pio.

In tear-streaked faces that reflect raw pain, in smiles that mask the same, we implore the soothing balm of the Most Powerful Healing Prayers.

With frail hands that tremble, with strong ones that offer their support, we reach out for God's abundant grace.

Through tear-blurred eyes that see life's fragility, through clear ones that behold joy in spite, we venerate the power of God's mercy.

In the presence of family and friends who love, in the absence of those beyond reach, St. Padre Pio, accompany us in prayer.

In shared meals that nourish, in missed ones that remind of every loss, shower upon us the sustenance of the Most Powerful Healing Prayers.

In the power of medical science, in its inevitable limits, we entrust our hope to God, the Ultimate Healer.

In life's fleeting moments that feel eternal, in its enduring ones that vanish too swiftly, we cherish the timeless bond of God's love.

In the tug of fear that unsettles, in the embrace of faith that upholds, we invoke your intercession, St. Padre Pio.

In the anguish of uncertainty, in fleeting moments of clarity, we long for the promise of God's healing peace.

In the solitude of the night, in the bustling light of day, we find solace in God's unfailing presence.

In our fervent yearning for healing, in our resignation to His will, we submit ourselves to His divine plan.

In our earthly journey fraught with trials, in our path toward eternal peace, St. Padre Pio, aid us with the Most Powerful Healing Prayers.

In our fleeting moments of fear, in our lifetime of faith, we fortify ourselves with God's everlasting strength.

In our silent prayers of the soul, in our voiced pleas for serenity, we implore God's consoling mercy.

In the balm of kind words, in the sting of painful truths, we trust in His healing wisdom.

For in the hospice halls and beyond, in life's every corner and its expansive center, we continue to seek your intercession, St. Padre Pio.

For in the love we share, in the pain we bear, we place our faith in the Most Powerful Healing Prayers. And in our every breath and pause, in our every sigh and relief, we acknowledge the omnipotent architect of our lives, God.

Prayer against Insomnia

St. Padre Pio, intercede on our behalf, who are voyagers on the tumultuous seas of restlessness. Those of us who lie awake in an overbearing silence, plagued by the famine of tranquil sleep. Each pendulum swing of the moon our spirit cries out, our bodies lack the necessary rest, the ordained peace of the night.

O great St. Pio, who bore the wounds of Christ, let your healing intercession be our solace in this dreary twilight of insomnia. In this night of a thousand blinking stars, beseech for us the Lover of Souls, to beat away this persisting storm of wakefulness and allow us to lie down in restful slumber.

From your throne of humility beseech, for us who are wearied and worn, the gift of peaceful dreams painted on the canvas of celestial night. May the Divine Musician strum holy lullabies upon the strings of our restive souls, cradling our beings to the soothing rhythm of His love.

Harbor Master of repose, plead for us who are held captive in the chains of unrest. May the Holy Spirit, the Comforter, soothe our inner turmoil, as a balmy zephyr quiets the tempestuous sea. Evaporate from our hearts this mist of anxiety, and ignite within us the liberating glow of faith.

Intercede, our saintly beacon, in the cosmic expanse of our wakeful nights. Let the Sea Weaver cast His sacred net, teeming with bountiful serenity, hauling us back to the shores of peaceful slumber. To dwell in the calm waters of His divine presence, nourished by the bread of serenity and the wine of tranquility.

Radiant beacon of divine intercession, invoke for us who wander through this desert of restlessness, the oasis of serenity. May our burdens be lightened, our spirits renewed, and our shadows of torment replaced by dawns of hope.

Mystic navigator, guide us through this odyssey of bleary wakefulness. Lead us back to the haven of deep sleep, where dreams flow like fresh streams from the mountains of divine providence, and our souls are blanketed in the silent serenity of the night.

In earnest supplication we pray, O Padre Pio, for the soothing balm of calmness and the reassuring whisper of hope. Set our sails towards the Island of Dreams, illuminated by the bright beacon of the Divine Lighthouse. Unfurl the sails of our trust in His word, that we may break free from the bondage of tormenting insomnia.

St Padre Pio, intercede for us, as we seek solace, not in the fleeting sands of earthly solutions, but in the depth of divine tranquillity. Anchor us in the safe being of the Almighty, that each night becomes a nurturing womb, nursing us to the health of a peaceful sleep, and leading us to wake refreshed, ready to serve with energy, love and delight.

May the God of peace endow us with His strength, His courage, His hope, and His love. For we are all travelers on this sea of life, reliant on the Divine Captain, compelled by His grace, guided by His steadfast lighthouse. Amen.

Prayer for Harmony in Body and Soul

Dearest Lord Jesus, I humbly approach You, my eyes glistening with tears and heart heavy with the weight of my frailty. My weariness is vast, my aches are real. There exists disarray within me, my spirit yearns for harmony, my body longs for relief.

Glorious Saint Padre Pio, bearer of the wounds of Christ, your life a testament of astounding miracles. I ask for your intercession right now. I trust in your holy communion with our loving Savior, your fervent prayers like incense reaching the throne of grace.

I look upon my body, a vessel of mortal clay, marred by afflictions. I see the inference of sickness, weariness it inflicts upon me. Yet in this humble vessel, I seek a healing only the Divine Healer can bestow. Bless my body, O Lord, let your healing hand rest upon me.

In the quiet sanctuary of my soul, turmoil stirs. I ask for your peace, O Lord, the peace that surpasses all understanding. Harmonize the melodies of my being, tune the strings of my spirit and make me resonate with your celestial chord. Invoke calm within the currents of my thoughts, in the ebb and flow of my desires, restore serenity within my soul.

I offer my pain, my discomfort, my affliction unto you, O Christ. Let them be a silent prayer. Purify them in your divine fire, transform them into carriers of your grace. Like Saint Pio who bore your wounds, may my suffering unite me closer to you.

In my infirmities, I find strength in You, most Sacred Heart. In my anguish, I see the possibilities for greater compassion.

In my pain, I am drawn into the mystery of Your suffering. Take my hand, O Divine Healer, lead me in this echoing valley of silence and suffering, towards the dawn of your promised healing.

Divine Physician, be my solace, be my refuge. Allow the blessings of Saint Padre Pio's intercession to saturate every cell, every fiber of my being. Let the power of his holy prayers course like a river within me, healing, restoring, renewing.

On the mountaintop I sing your praise, in the valley I find your presence. In every beating of my heart, every breath drawn, every pain suffered, may I encounter You, the Source of Life and Healing.

St. Padre Pio, I thank you for your heavenly intercession. Continue to pray for me, that I may have the grace to accept whatever comes. As you partook in the fellowship of our Lord's sufferings, intercede for me that I might find solace in the midst of my trials, healing in my moments of pain, and harmony within my body and soul.

Lord Jesus, in the sacrament of the ailing, soothe me, sanctify me, bless me with a healing that is more than the absence of affliction but the presence of profound peace. This I pray, trusting in your tender mercies and St. Padre Pio's strenuous intercession. Amen.

Prayer for Respite from Trauma

Healing Father, inspire us with the healing prayers of St. Padre Pio; let their power permeate our broken spirit. In our struggle and suffering, we seek the comfort of Your divine grace.

In the face of trauma, we falter; we stumble; we ache; through the intercession of St. Padre Pio, we pray for strength. The human spirit is fragile, set easily adrift by the assaults of life; yet, in You, we find resilience.

In the shadow of our pain, we tremble; we fear; we doubt; through the intercession of St. Padre Pio, hope rises, a beacon in our darkened world. The human heart is susceptible, often overwhelmed by the tribulations of existence; still, in Your love, we discover solace.

In the aftermath of our trials, we question; we agonize; we despair; through the intercession of St. Padre Pio, tranquillity descends, a balm for our troubled souls. The human mind reels, lost in the mazes of despair; nevertheless, in Your wisdom, we discern clarity.

Resilience, solace, and clarity, gifts of Your divine love; our petition, sincere and earnest, seeks Your profound comfort. St Padre Pio, intercede for us, bring the power of healing prayers into our lives, infuse our spirits with vitality.

In our sorrow, Your consoling embrace; in our pain, Your soothing touch; in our despair, Your inspiring whisper. Bound to mortality, we find ourselves frail; yet, bound to You, we find ourselves strong.

Oh Healing Father, in our adversity, turn our hearts towards You; in our fear, encourage our faith; in our doubt, foster our certainty. Through the intercession of St. Padre Pio, we seek not to avoid our trials but to find you amidst them.

In our misery, there is hope; in our suffering, there is peace; in our pain, there is healing. We accept our human frailty, embracing our divine potential; in our weakness, we stand strong; in our sorrows, we endure, always striving towards You.

May our pleas for healing resonate, echoing through the firmament, reverberating through the hearts of the suffering. Through the intercession of St. Padre Pio, may Your radiant love heal the deepest wounds of our hearts.

Healing Father, in the face of trauma, remind us of our constant truth: we are not alone; You are with us even in the deepest corners of our struggle. Through the intercession of St. Padre Pio, may we experience Your most profound healing, transforming our despair into a resolute hope, our fear into courageous faith, our pain into enduring strength.

Trusting in Your divine love and guided by the prayers of St. Padre Pio, we pray for healing, for peace, for resilience. In the darkest nights of our souls, may Your love be the dawn that breaks, bringing respite and illuminating our path towards healing; Amen.

Prayer for Cleansing of Negativity

In the name of Jesus Christ, our Lord and Savior, we beseech Thee, St. Padre Pio;

Intercede for us at the Throne of Grace.

We believe in Thy power to heal body, soul and spirit;

A power bestowed by the Almighty Father.

We humbly lay before Thee our plea for healing;

Release from the burdens of negativity.

Through your intercession, may Divine Healing reign upon us;

The Healing power of Christ which transcends all earthly ailment.

We ask for the obstruction of negative energy be lifted;

We earnestly seek freedom from the chains of discontent.

Grant us a heart receptive to the whispers of God;

St. Padre Pio, cleanse our hearts from all unfounded fear.

We decree purity of mind, openness of heart;

Apathy, scorn and disdain, be vanquished in the mighty name of Jesus.

Through St. Padre Pio's intercession we yearn for healing;

Radiating from the loving heart of the Father Almighty.

We believe in His power to mend, to restore, to rejuvenate;

Let His perfect will and immense love envelop us.

We adhere to the sacred assurance of deliverance;

From the clutches of negativity that abound.

We strongly profess in the great harmony of His love;

His love that overpowers any form of negativism.

May His mercy cleanse our souls, our minds, our hearts;

From negative thoughts, negative words and negative actions.

In this act of faith, we seek your intercession St. Padre Pio;

Simply that we may live in the fullness of the Father's love.

With a spirit emboldened by His ceaseless mercy;

There shall not be room for the negative, only His lasting peace.

Our Redeemer's blood purifies us; refines us;

And thus we shall radiate His divine goodness, His profound love.

St. Padre Pio, intercede for us, make us worthy of His Grace;

In our journey, may we uphold His will and His word.

We implore you, stand with us, guide us, and guard us;

Until we claim our healing and live solely in the Light of Christ.

In the potent name of Jesus, our sovereign Redeemer;

St. Padre Pio, we beseech your intersession. Amen.

Prayer for Hope in Turmoil

Oh Saint Padre Pio, oriented towards God's mercy, help me in this turmoil. Guide my heart towards hope, away from despair. Let me cry when tears cleanse and laugh when joy heals. Let me lean into the wind of the storm, even when my body is weak.

Oh St. Padre Pio, bring me to the depths of my soul, where healing resides. Let me shatter barriers and breathe freely. Let me cast off heavy chains and float in Your grace. Let me abandon darkness and embrace the beacon of love.

Let me imagine pain as a cornerstone, not detriment, to my journey towards God. Let me perceive suffering as a bridge to transcendence, rather than an end. Let me understand torment as a challenge, not an everlasting curse.

Oh St. Padre Pio, gift me the sight of the divine within my wounds. Let me observe divine grace even in my plight. Let me identify divinity in my own aching humanity. Let me recognize the sacred in the depths of my desolation.

Let my voice rise from the abyss, articulated with courage and faith. Let my whimpers turn into battle cries for hope. Let my whisperings of despair transform into resounding affirmations of resilience. Let my utterances of doubt become declarations of steadfast trust.

Oh St. Padre Pio, let the divine energy charge every cell in my body. Let me harness the celestial power in every breath, and in every heartbeat. Let me be a conduit of divine healing energy, healing myself, healing others.

Through your intercession, St. Padre Pio, let me cultivate understanding within my suffering. Let me not detach from pain, but to feel it, to learn from it, to grow in it. Let me see how turmoil carves space in my soul for greater courage, deeper compassion, and undying hope.

Let me, in my darkest hour, remember the grace of God's healing hand. Let me, in my weakest moment, find strength through divine communion. Let me, in my pain, find the path to hope, guided by Your merciful gaze.

Oh St. Padre Pio, as I walk through the valley of sorrow, arm me with resilience. Let me not falter before the shadows, but to stand tall, radiant in God's glory. Let me recite the most powerful healing prayers, with unwavering conviction, fervid passion, and relentless hope.

Among the ashes of turmoil, let me be the phoenix, rising, glowing, healed. Hear my prayer, Oh St. Padre Pio, and carry it into the divine presence, bolstering my hope amidst the turmoil. You who understood suffering, be my guide, my healer, my beacon. Through your blessed intercession, may divine healing grace be mine. Amen.

Prayer for Renewal

St. Padre Pio, Servant of God, I come before you in humility and faith.

You, who carried the stigmata of Christ, you who bore His pain, extend to us your healing hands.

You, who felt the weight of the cross, understand our burdens and our bodily afflictions.

We beseech you, St. Padre Pio, intercede for us, bring our cries of pain before the Most High.

With you, dear Saint, we trust in the love and mercy of God, the ultimate source of our healing.

With you, we believe that God hears our humble pleas, sees our physical and spiritual suffering.

St. Padre Pio, kneel with us in prayer, hold us close when we are weak and weary.

Let your compassion give us hope, let your intercession bring us comfort.

Christ, Healer of all, hear us through St. Padre Pio's intercession.

Christ, Redeemer of the world, renew us in body, spirit, and mind.

Christ, Compassionate One, ease our pain, restore our strength.

Christ, Prince of Peace, quiet our fears, calm our troubled hearts.

Christ, Divine Physician, work your miracles of healing within us.

For those of us bedridden, Christ, restore our vitality.

For those of us writhing in pain, Christ, alleviate our suffering.

For those of us grappling with terminal illnesses, Christ, extend your hand of healing.

For those battling mental affliction, Christ, grant clarity of mind and peace of heart.

Through St. Padre Pio's intercession, Christ, renew us.

Renew our faith in You, renew our hope in Your divine mercy.

By Your wounds, may our wounds be healed.

By Your death, may our lives be renewed.

And though we walk through the valley of sickness, we will not be afraid, for You are with us.

Through the prayers of St. Padre Pio, we hold on to Your promise of healing and renewal.

In Your mercy, Christ, receive our plea.

In Your love, Christ, answer our call.

Through the intercession of St. Padre Pio, may we experience Your most powerful healing.

Christ, have mercy on us.

Christ, heal and renew us.

Amen.

Thank you Lord...

Padre Pio, please intercede for me...

My personal prayer...

My prayer for my loved ones...

My current challenges...

Lord, offer me guidance...

Novena

Introduction

As we embark on this nine-day spiritual journey in search of healing, we turn towards the extraordinary life and faith of St. Padre Pio as our guiding path. This novena serves not merely as a sequence of prayers but a transformative pilgrimage to aid us in navigating our trials. Together, we shall traverse a path of deep reflection, embracing the peace and strength that these powerful verses can bestow.

St. Padre Pio, renowned for his exceptional spirituality and miraculous gifts, devoted his life to serving God and those in pain. His extraordinary, unflinching faith took him on a divine journey that we now revisit in a bid to unveil our own spiritual enlightenment.

Each day focuses on a unique chapter of St. Padre Pio's life, immersing us in his profound sense of prayer, healing, and the miraculous. From his humble beginnings to his ascension into sainthood, we will reflect upon his life to cultivate a closer bond with God and to guide our drive towards resilience and serenity.

As we step onto this path bolstered by St. Padre Pio's fervent prayers, may this novena serve as a beacon, guiding us towards the sanctuary of healing. We embark on this profound journey with hope and faith, assured that St. Padre Pio's ever-pervading spirit is with us, guiding and inspiring us to seek the powerful harmony that comes with genuine healing. Let us embrace this novena as a vessel carrying us towards that divine embrace of restorative serenity.

Thank you Lord for...

_____
_____
_____
_____
_____
_____
_____
_____
_____
_____
_____
_____
_____
_____

My personal novena intentions...

_____
_____
_____
_____
_____
_____
_____
_____
_____
_____
_____
_____
_____
_____
_____
_____
_____
_____

My intentions for humanity...

My novena intentions for my loved ones...

First Day

Born on May 25, 1887, in Pietrelcina, Italy, into a humble and religious family, St. Padre Pio, originally known as Francesco Forgione, felt the divine calling early. At the tender age of five, young Francesco reportedly had celestial visions and communicated with Jesus and Mary. Recognizing his exceptional spiritual sensitivity, Francesco's parents nurtured his faith, aiding his journey toward the priesthood.

Close your eyes, dear reader, and imagine a field in Pietrelcina, bathed in the golden light of setting sun. Visualize a young Francesco, treading softly among the tall blades of grass, his lips whispering prayers as his heart danced with divine love.

"Gracious God, following the path illuminated by Your Holy Light, guide me toward healing. Lead me away from my physical and spiritual sufferings, just as you guided St. Padre Pio in his lifetime."

Though born into a humble setting, Francesco was rich in faith. That faith, mixed with the hardships of his material existence, prepared him for divine service. At fifteen, stepping up to his commitment to God, Francesco joined the Order of Friars Minor Capuchin and took the name 'Pio.' He was ordained a priest eight years later, forever embracing his role as a spiritual healer and guide.

"Lord, just as you embraced young Pio into Your service, embrace me in Your healing arms. Infuse me with the strength to persevere through my struggles and to trust in Your Divine Plan."

St. Padre Pio's lieutenant life was marked by hardship. His health was poor, and he bore the Stigmata - the wounds of Jesus' crucifixion - only a few years into his priesthood. Yet, he drew strength from his devotion, prayer, and zealous service to God and mankind.

"Almighty God, as Your humble servant St. Padre Pio bore suffering with courage and faith, help me bear my trials with the same grace. Inspire me with a spirit of endurance to face the storms of life and to find peace amidst them."

Gazing onto the path of St. Padre Pio's early life, we recognize a pattern of humility, faith, and piety. Swallowed in prayer and dedicated to divine service, St. Pio turned pain into purpose, transforming suffering into a means of salvation.

We, too, can find solace and healing in prayer, just as St. Pio did. Let us, therefore, emulate his faith, praying not just for ourselves, but for the healing of others, too.

"Beloved God, allow me to echo the faith of St. Padre Pio. Lead me towards a path of healing, not just for myself but for others, too. As St. Pio transformed suffering into service, let my trials be a means of living out Your will."

As we embark on this first day of our novena, let us carry the early life of St. Padre Pio with us, imitating his humble yet strong faith, his devotion, and his commitment to service through trials and suffering.

Second Day

In today's meditation, we focus on the calling of St. Padre Pio, his unyielding faith, and how his deep spirituality sustained him during challenging periods of his life. Let us embrace the profound wisdom of St. Padre Pio and endeavor to earnestly apply his teachings of love, faith, and perseverance in our daily lives.

St. Padre Pio valued prayer, often equating it with oxygen, the very breath of life. He once said, "Prayer is the best weapon we have; it is the key to God's heart. You must speak to Jesus not only with your lips, but with your heart." This belief was intrinsic in his faith journey and formed the foundation of his ability to perform miraculous healings. It was in his devout prayer life that he fostered an intimate relationship with Jesus, allowing him to become a vessel of divine healing.

St. Padre Pio's calling came to him at a tender age and he dedicated his life to the service of Jesus Christ. He plunged into this spiritual path with enthusiasm and devotion, seeking to practice a humble and unselfish love. However, the path wasn't easy. He encountered many hardships and was even subjected to skepticism and ridicule from those around him. Despite these cynics, St. Padre Pio remained steadfast, drawing strength from his intense prayer life.

This profound spirituality was evident when he received the stigmata, the wounds of Christ, marking him as uniquely chosen by God. St. Padre Pio experienced these supernatural phenomena, not with fanfare, but with humility, accepting these divine markings as opportunities to identify further with the sufferings of Jesus.

St. Padre Pio displayed an unwavering commitment to prayer and spirituality, affirming his belief in divine power and healing. Owing to his relentless pursuit of God, many flocked to him, seeking spiritual guidance, healing, and reconciliation. Known for his power of discernment, he often knew the sins of the penitents even before they confessed, acting as a divine instrument of grace and mercy.

Let us reflect on our own spiritual journey, considering the challenges we face and the skepticism we might have met. Are there moments we doubted ourselves or God's vocation? Do we spend thoughtful time in prayer, nurturing our relationship with Jesus, and seeking guidance?

These are questions that might not always have immediately clear answers. But today, inspired by the life of St. Padre Pio, let us take a moment to evaluate our spiritual path, recommit to a life of prayer, and acknowledge that God's divine healing can flow through us, as intermediaries of His love and mercy.

Today's prayer focuses on choosing faith over doubt, prayer over despair, and service over self. We pray for divine strength to soldier on in our spiritual journey, just like St. Padre Pio, trusting in God's infinite mercy and healing powers.

Heavenly Father, we beseech your guidance and divine healing. Encourage us to hold firm to our faith, like your faithful servant, St. Padre Pio. Through his intercession, may we nurture our relationship with You, deepen our commitment to prayer, and mirror his spiritual ardor, thus experiencing Your profound healing. Amen.

Third Day

Let us begin this day of our novena with a recognition of the palpable devotion St. Padre Pio possessed throughout his life. From an early age, the pull towards a spiritual life was irresistible to him, a calling he accepted with humility and unwavering commitment. As a friar at the Capuchin monastery, his faith was tested time and time again, yet his devotion to God remained firm, even in times of great turmoil and strife.

His life and work at the monastery, whether it was through his participation in the Liturgy, the Sacrament of Penance or his spiritual direction, bore testimony to his deep connection with God. St. Padre Pio was known for his diligent and fervent prayer life, a pillar that sustained him in times of trial and nourished his closeness to God. So fervent was his prayer life, that it's been recounted his prayers had the power to open up the heavens, inciting divine intervention for numerous cases deemed hopeless by human standards.

St. Padre Pio, we ask you to guide us on this third day of our novena as we strive to build a deeper connection with God, much like you did during your time on earth. We yearn for an unwavering faith, a trust so deep that it can withstand the storms that may strive to shake our belief. Show us the path to fervent prayer and deliverance, the path to steadfast faith and profound devotion that opens our hearts to divine love, grace, and forgiveness.

Please pray for us, St. Padre Pio, that we may learn to embody your devotion and faithfulness in service to God. May we, through your guidance in prayer, learn to humbly accept our own trials and tribulations, and find comfort in the omnibenevolent embrace of our heavenly Father.

Just as suffering led you to a deeper connection with Christ, we wish to transform our struggles into stepping stones towards spiritual enlightenment, and gain solace through our intimate relationship with the Almighty. As we pray, help us to feel His presence, His warmth, and His love wrapped around us - a profound reassurance that allows us to press forward, armed by faith.

St. Padre Pio, we implore you to aid us in our journey. As we immerse ourselves in prayer, allow us to experience the same divine communion that graced your life. Just as you did, let us serve as vessels through which the Lord's work may be accomplished, and in doing so, find our own path to healing and wholeness.

Impart on us your resolute spirit in the face of adversity, the strength of your faith despite the enormity of the trials you bore. Pray for us, St. Padre Pio, that we too may discover the transformative power of prayer, the peace that comes from surrendering our burdens to God and finding solace in His eternal, comforting embrace.

In this journey of reconnecting with our faith, we ask for your intercession, St. Padre Pio - shape us with your strength, inspire us with your unwavering faith, and guide us with your profound devotion, so that we continually draw closer to God. Amen.

Fourth Day

Reflecting upon this unique phase in Padre Pio's life, where he graduated from novice to priest, helps us to grasp the immense dedication and obedience he embodied. He was a man of great faith, who chose to dedicate his life to the service of mankind and the greater glory of our Lord. As we immerse ourselves in this day of novena, let's perceive his transformation as an inspiration for our spiritual journey towards healing and tranquility.

Let us pray:

In the name of the Father, the Son, and the Holy Spirit, Amen.

Dear Lord, we thank you for the profound gift of Padre Pio's priesthood; for his selfless commitment in bringing so near to us Your abundant graces, Your merciful love, and the transfiguring power of the Holy Mass. His devotion to the priesthood was a testament to the divine healing power You have bestowed upon those You have chosen.

Today, as we commemorate Padre Pio's commitment, let us aspire to uphold a resolve as firm as his in our journey toward healing. We humbly ask you to empower us, to heal us, and to enlighten us in our times of trials and tribulations. As St. Padre Pio turned to You in every moment - in joy, in sorrow, in trial, and in victory, guide us, o Loving Father, to do the same.

We remember the holy Masses Padre Pio celebrated, how he transcended the boundaries of the earthly realm to unite us with You. He spoke not with words, but through the silent language of sacrificial love, becoming a beacon of hope for the distressed and the ailing. Let this memory move us to appreciate every celebration of the Holy Eucharist as an opportunity for healing, nourishment, and communion with You.

Lord, allow us to understand that every struggle we face is a call to turn closer to You, just as Padre Pio did. Let us see every challenge as a stepping stone toward spiritual growth and enlightenment. Imbue us with the everlasting faith of St. Padre Pio. Encourage our hearts to trust in You, to yield to Your divine will, and to find solace in Your loving embrace.

Paths of earthly life confuse and challenge us. When we totter, let us cling upon the life of Padre Pio, his faith, his sacrifices, and his undying love for You. In his words, "Pray, Hope, and Don't Worry" let these become our mantra when we navigate through the ambiguities of life.

Through the intercession of St. Padre Pio, we pray for the grace to be selfless, to carry our crosses daily, and to trust in Your divine providence and healing. As we near the halfway mark of this novena, enlighten us, Almighty Father, to profoundly comprehend the life of St. Padre Pio and the healing power of a prayerful life.

Glory be to the Father, to the Son, and to the Holy Spirit, as it was in the beginning, is now, and forever will be, world without end.

St. Padre Pio, Pray for Us.

Amen.

Bask in the divine grace of this novena day and let its blessings facilitate your journey of healing and spiritual growth. Embrace the directions of the Holy Spirit and delve into the profound essence of this day.

Fifth Day

Let us embark on this day with a prayer:

Heavenly Father, as we contemplate the life of Your faithful servant, St. Padre Pio, inspire within us the strength to accept Your divine will as he did. In our moments of trials and uncertainties, echo within us the words of Padre Pio: "Pray, hope and don't worry. God is merciful and hears our prayers."

St. Padre Pio, a beacon of unwavering courage and faith, lived each day of his life surrendered to God's will. He believed every trial he bore, even the ineffable pain of his stigmata, to be a divine journey, a path leading him closer to God. Each pain borne and every struggle weathered were accepted as holy offerings, acts of love rendered to his Divine Beloved.

Today, in this novena, we focus on this brave acceptance by St. Padre Pio. His submission to God's will was not a passive resignation, but an active engagement. He accepted God's will, not with hesitancy or fear, but in an utmost spirit of faith and reverence. He saw his trials as opportunities, using them to cultivate a deeper sense of compassion and humility. His sufferings became transformative experiences which drew him closer to God and to his fellowmen.

Life is complicated and full of uncertainties. However, Padre Pio invites us to live our lives with serene acceptance and resolute bravery - not to rid our lives of struggles, but to face them with faith, courage, and unyielding grace. To follow the path Padre Pio walked is to accept that we too may have our own trials, our own crosses to bear, and yet it is also to trust in the healing, restorative power of God's divine will.

As we pray this novena, may we not lose sight of this invitation to growth and deepening faith. With each word uttered, let us invite in the spirit of bravery that St. Padre Pio embodied, trusting in God's plan and accepting His will as our sanctifying guide amidst the turbulence of this earthly life.

Let us now pray:

St. Padre Pio, in times of trial and hard times, help us to embrace the divine will of the Father just as you embraced your stigmata. In insignificant moments of worry or monumental times of stress, remind us to pray, hope, and not worry, echoing your faithful words to those near you.

May our hearts be filled with the grace to accept our trials as part of our spiritual journey. Guide us to see them not as obstacles but as stepping stones leading us closer to our Father. May we bear them with courage, humility, and love for God's will.

Today we pray to embrace the divine will of God in our lives, with the faith and fortitude of St. Padre Pio. This we ask in the sweet and glorious name of Jesus Christ our Lord.

St. Padre Pio, pray for us. Amen.

Sixth Day

Let us, on this sixth day, ponder upon the miracles that manifest in the form of physical wounds mimicking those of Christ; the Stigmata, which was miraculously gifted to St. Padre Pio. We are reminded of his faith, so powerful, so surmountable, that it inscribed itself on his very flesh, marking a testament to his unwavering devotion. We offer our intentions today in the hope that we too may be imbued with a faith as resolute, a spirit as steadfast, while we seek healing and spiritual enlightenment.

In silence, we contemplate the magnitude of St. Padre Pio's faith and devotion. The manifestations of stigmata were not only outward symbols but were testaments of his inward sanctity. He bore these wounds with humility, accepting the intense torment not as punishment, but as participation in Christ's suffering. Yet, miraculously, his wounds never became infected, nor did they deteriorate his health, proving that they were indeed a Divine occurrence.

St. Padre Pio, we pray, instill in us the same devotion you showed throughout your life. Guide us in our journey towards healing, giving us not only the strength to bear our wounds but also the faith to see them as opportunities to participate in Christ's suffering.

Through your intercession, St. Padre Pio, we ask for the courage to face our personal hardships. Like you, may we recognize our wounds as symbols of our own path to enlightenment. And in carrying these burdens, may we become closer to Christ and find solace in His divine love.

As we reflect upon your life, St. Padre Pio, we acknowledge that you were a man of miracles. Through Christ, you cured the sick, the lost, and the wounded. We humbly ask today that we, too, may become a conduit of His miraculous works of healing. Help us to bring Christ's love to the broken, to be beacons of hope in this world of uncertainty.

Through your example, we learn that faith is a profound power, capable of manifesting miracles in our lives. As such, we pray for undying faith amid our adversities. We beseech God, through your intercession, to grant us everlasting hope, the strength of spirit, and the peace of heart to overcome our personal battles.

Today, we internalize your words, St. Padre Pio: "Prayer is the best weapon we possess. It is the key that opens God's heart." We vow to arm ourselves with this powerful weapon, ensuring that every step we take towards healing is grounded in prayer and faith.

To those fighting their battles, we dedicate this day's prayer to you. May the Lord, through the intercession of St. Padre Pio, hear your pleas and relieve you from your suffering.

May we, like St. Padre Pio, infused with the Spirit, bear our trials with grace, seeing in them a pathway to divine intervention. Amen.

As we conclude this day's reflection and prayer, we make a spiritual communion with St. Padre Pio, earnestly yearning for the faith that marked his commitment to Christ and seeking the miracles of healing that his faith brought forth. Let this inspire us to deepen our faith and trust in God's divine providence, even amid sufferings and trials. Amen.

Seventh Day

We commence this day with the embodiment of St. Padre Pio's humility in our hearts, and strive to mirror his austere lifestyle and abundant devotion in our actions. Known for his modest existence and profuse love for God, Padre Pio showed us that the path to true healing and spiritual enlightenment lies in embracing simplicity and maintaining an unwavering bond with the divine.

In emulating St. Padre Pio, we begin by temporarily casting aside our obsession with earthly achievements and possessions. We detach ourselves from the glimmering distractions of the material realm and strive to convert our acquisitive instinct into an aspiring journey towards the spiritual dimension. We recognize the transitory charm of earthly treasures, and yearn for the everlasting bliss that lies in God's love and grace.

Today, as we proceed in our Novena, let us contemplate on these words, attributed to Padre Pio: "Do not fear. Jesus is more powerful than all hell."

In the quiet sanctity of this moment, we embrace the strength of these words. We understand that our fears and worries are mere trivialities in the face of God's love, strength and protection. Embracing the spiritual depth and divine truth in these powerful words, we let the light of faith dissolve our doubts and fears.

Padre Pio, we seek your intercession on this blessed day. As we strive to honor your life by emulating your devotion, empower our spirit to steadfastly resist worldly allurements. Impart upon us the discernment to prefer spiritual treasures above transient worldly ones. Propel us towards the path that cultivates virtues and kindles within us an unquenchable thirst for divine love and grace.

We invite you, oh St. Padre Pio, to graciously share with us your wisdom, guide our thoughts, and help us cultivate a heart of service, echoing your life's devotion to God and sharing in your divine love for the least, the last, and the lost.

As we continue to immerse ourselves in fervent prayer, we implore your intercession to seek not the ephemeral solace of worldly treasures, but the everlasting light and warmth of God's love and grace. Help us undeniably believe, like you did, that no dark force can overshadow God's powerful light, which can guide us on our path towards healing and spiritual enlightenment.

Today, our hearts are filled with humility and reverence, as we seek to emulate your noble life. St. Padre Pio, help us model our lives on yours, shunning worldly desires and prioritizing a life of spiritual engagements. Enlighten our minds to absorb the profound wisdom that lies in simple, virtuous living and relentless, loving devotion to God.

In faith and hope, we pray. Amen.

As we goodbye to this day of our Novena, let us carry forward the lessons we've amassed – the richness of a humble life, the power of unwavering faith in God, and the healing potential of a profoundly devoted spiritual journey. May we follow the footprints of St Padre Pio in our quest for spiritual enlightenment and infinite healing. Amen.

Eighth Day

Let us begin with our invocation, calling upon the loving presence of St. Padre Pio.

"St. Padre Pio, through your unconditional love, you became a beacon of charity, of compassion for the ailing and the suffering. We revere your unfaltering faith and the determination with which you accepted the stigmata, proclaiming by your actions the limitless power of Jesus Christ's divine mercy. Now, we humbly turn our hearts and our intentions to you, asking for comfort, for healing, and for a heart filled with compassion, akin to yours."

Begin your reflection by imagining the life of St. Padre Pio, focusing particularly on his long hours attending to the wounded and suffering. Visualize the deep empathy radiating from his eyes, feel his unyielding hands, which, despite the painful wounds, extended aid and kindness to the sick and needy.

As we meditate, we silently pray: "Lord, imbue in us the essence of St. Padre Pio's spirit, especially his boundless capacity for empathy and his desire to alleviate suffering. Grant us the strength to endure our own afflictions while offering comfort to others in their time of need."

Then, with the compassionate spirit of St. Padre Pio in our minds, pray the following:

"St. Padre Pio, we beseech your intercession today, asking for the fortitude to live in service to others as you did. Bestow upon us the strength to carry our crosses, as well as your wisdom in assisting and understanding the crosses borne by others. May the uncompromising love and mercy you portrayed help us to see more clearly God's divine plan, and may the sacrifices you made inspire us to live in accord with His holy will.

"Eternal Father, instill in us the same fervent love for the Eucharist that fired the heart of St. Padre Pio. May it be a font of comfort, sustenance, and healing for our bodies and souls. Through our communion, may we be united with you and with all our brothers and sisters in Christ who bear the weight of suffering in this life."

"For all those battling physical, mental, or emotional pain, we seek your divine intervention, St. Padre Pio. Be their beacon of hope in their darkest hours, guiding them towards the comforting rays of Christ's love."

"Help us to remember, O Beloved Healer, that wounds and suffering are not merely physical afflictions, but spiritual opportunities. Like the stigmata that you bore with unwavering faith, may we see our own wounds as symbols of Christ's own suffering, and as connections to His profound act of love."

"Through our suffering, patient endurance, and through your divine intercession, St. Padre Pio, may we embrace the healing power of compassion and prayer. May we, like you, become instruments of God's infinite mercy, showering His love and peace upon those around us."

We conclude today's reflection with the firm resolution to live in the spirit of St. Padre Pio, upholding his tenets of compassion, mindfulness, and unflinching faith. Ask the Lord to nourish these desires in our hearts and to provide us the strength and understanding necessary to fulfil our mission in this world. Amen.

Ninth Day

Let us begin our meditation today by recalibrating our weary souls and minds, setting them on the serene landscape of St. Padre Pio's sacred journey. As we seek to intertwine our paths with the spiritual wisdom illuminated by this saint, we open our hearts to divine intervention and spiritual healing that surpass our understanding.

St. Padre Pio, a humble friar, who through his blessed life, bore the wounds of Christ, deepening his spiritual devotion and alignment with the divine healing power. By contemplating his lifelong dedication, we find endless reservoirs of courage to face our own battles, the turmoil that questions our faith, and the diseases that challenge our physical and mental fortitude.

O beloved Saint, we humbly request you as our heavenly intercessor, to implore the divine mercy of God to touch those areas of our lives that are wounded. We beseech the grace that flowed from your saintly life, the grace that made you a beacon of hope to those who sought your counsel, the grace that is able to restore physical and spiritual health.

Just like Job in the Bible, you trusted in God in spite of extreme pain and affliction. In moments of weakness and anguish, your profound faith and spiritual devotion shone through and paved the way for miracles. This imparts us with the belief that God's blessings and interventions are not restricted by earthly or materialistic perspectives - they are celestial, transformative, and capable of achieving what seems impossible to human eyes.

So often in life, we find ourselves weighed down by our crosses. Our bodies may fall ill, our minds may be troubled, and our spirits may suffer. Yet, through interceding for divine help through you, St. Padre Pio, we believe we can reach out to the healing touch of our Lord. We strive to emulate your devotion, seeking to understand the mysteries of God in the midst of pain, bathing in the showers of divine grace and consolation, and experiencing the miracles in the face of despair.

In blending our faith with your intercessory prayer, St. Padre Pio, we are reminded of God's unfailing presence in our lives. Though the struggles may seem unending, the pain unbearable, there is solace in knowing that we are not alone. You stand beside us as a testament to God's mercy.

Today, we conclude this novena journey by emphasizing our trust in God's healing power. St. Padre Pio, you remind us that we are not abandoned in our pain. Our prayers are heard. Our cries do resonate within the chambers of the divine. The path to healing may not be easy, it may not be short, but it is assured for those who hold steadfast faith and patience.

On this final day, dear St. Padre Pio, we sincerely thank you for guiding us on this spiritual journey. We implore you to continue praying for us, to help us embrace the power of healing, and to enrich us with the strength to carry our crosses with dignity and peace.

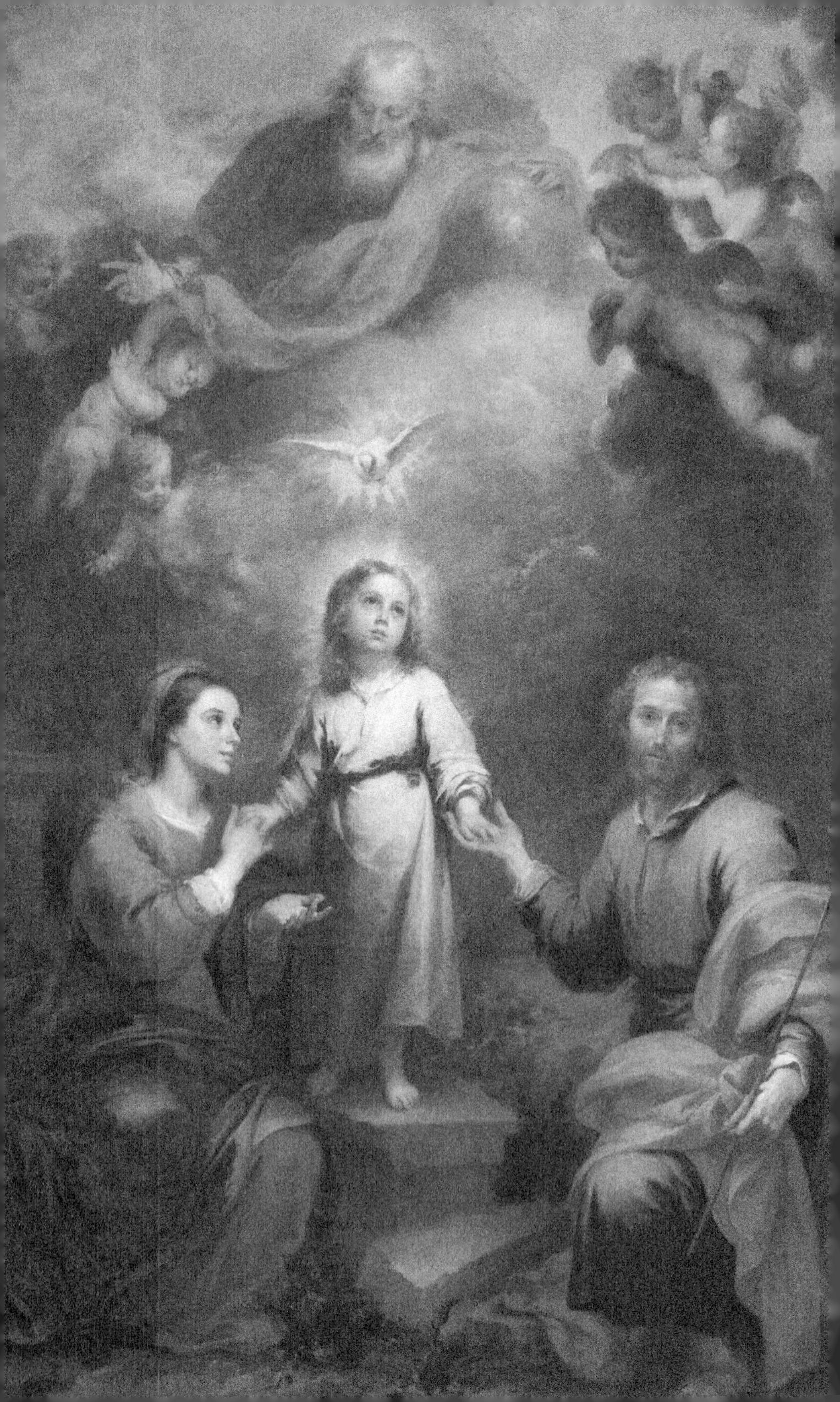

Thank you!

We greatly value your feedback on this book and invite you to share your thoughts directly with us. As a growing independent publishing company, we continuously aim to improve the quality of our publications.

For your convenience, the QR code below will lead you to our website. There, you can leave feedback directly to us or find the link to the Amazon review page to share your experience and offer any suggestions for improvement. On our website, you can also view our related books and access free supplementary materials.

Related books

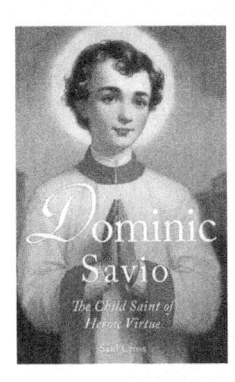

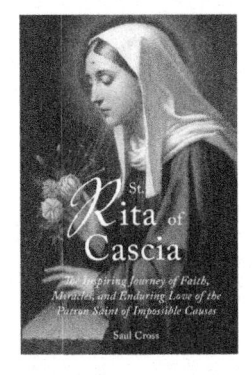